ABRAHAM LINCOLN

© **B. Jain Publishers (P) Ltd.** All rights reserved. No part of this book may be reproduced, stored in a retrieval system or transmitted, in any form or by any means, mechanical, photocopying, recording or otherwise, without any prior written permission of the publisher.

Published by Kuldeep Jain for B. Jain Publishers (P) Ltd., D-157, Sector 63, Noida - 201307, U.P
Registered office: 1921/10, Chuna Mandi, Paharganj, New Delhi-110055

Printed in India

Contents

5   Who was Abraham Lincoln?
6   Lincoln's Early Years
10   Left Alone in the Big World
17   The Turning Point
22   Moving Towards Success
31   The Skilled Debater
36   Election as President
40   A Divided Nation
46   End Of Slavery
50   The Gettysburg Address
53   The Victory
58   The Last Journey
60   Timeline
67   Activities
69   Glossary

Who was Abraham Lincoln?

Abraham Lincoln is regarded as one of the greatest heroes of American history due to both his incredible impact on the nation and his unique and distinctive appeal. His is a remarkable story of the rise from humble beginnings to achieve the highest office in the land; then, a sudden and tragic death at a time when his country needed him the most to complete the great task remaining before the nation.

It had shocked many when Lincoln overcame several more prominent contenders to win the Republican Party's nomination for president in 1860. Contrary to expectations, Lincoln proved to be a shrewd military strategist and a savvy leader during what became the costliest conflict ever fought on American soil. His Emancipation Proclamation, issued in 1863, freed all slaves in the rebellious states and paved the way for slavery's eventual abolition. His Gettysburg Address later that year stands as one of the most famous and influential pieces of oratory in American history. Over the years Lincoln's grand stature has only grown, and he is widely regarded as one of the greatest presidents in American history.

Lincoln's Early Years

Abraham Lincoln was born in a log cabin in Hardin County, Kentucky to Thomas Lincoln and Nancy Hanks Lincoln on February 12, 1809. Thomas was a strong and determined pioneer who found a moderate level of prosperity and was well respected in the community that he lived in. The couple had two other children, Abraham's older sister Sarah and younger brother Thomas who died in infancy.

Due to a dispute regarding some land, the Lincolns were forced to move from Kentucky to Perry County, Indiana in 1817, where the family occupied public land and began hunting game and farming on a small plot. Thomas Sr., eventually, was able to buy the land.

The area where they decided to live in was largely unsettled. The land was terribly overgrown and difficult to farm. Lincoln later described life in this area, known as Little Pigeon Creek, as 'a fight with trees logs and grubs'. While the family worked hard at farming, Thomas had to rely on hunting for most of the days in order to feed his family. Thomas eventually built a one-room cabin for the family but there was no flooring and little furniture.

family slept on corn husk beds that were plagued with bugs and rodents.

Their mother, Nancy, was very religious and taught the children about the Bible. She also believed in the importance of education. However, schools were uncommon in those areas. When Lincoln was about seven, a school opened nine miles away, and Nancy insisted her husband that the children should be allowed to attend. The walk to school would take the children almost three hours each way! However, the idea of going to school did not last long.

When Lincoln was nine, in the year 1818, Nancy became very ill with 'milk sickness', a disease which took her life. She passed away at the age of 34. Nancy's death left Sarah and Lincoln in the sole care of their father, who was too occupied by the need to hunt daily and to try to cultivate the land so they could grow food.

Historians often say that he was a tough man who was known to knock his son down in anger many a times. Lincoln grew more distant from his father and quietly resented the hard work placed on him at an early age.

Left Alone in the Big World

Sarah, aged 11, and Lincoln, aged 9, were heartbroken at losing their mother. The house was in a mess without Nancy. Tom, their poor father, realized that he needed help! So he left Lincoln and Sarah alone in the cabin while he returned to Kentucky to find a new wife. The children had little to eat other than dried berries that had been stored away by their late mother. A neighbour who stopped by reported that the children were terribly skinny, filthy, and the house was in a terrible condition.

Lincoln and Sarah were alone for half of the following year. They almost thought that they were abandoned. However, six months later, Thomas pulled up in a horse-drawn wagon with a new wife and her three children. Lincoln is said to have run to his new mother whom he had never met before and immediately bury his face in her skirts.

Lincoln's blind faith in her was well rewarded. Sarah Bush Johnston was a loving person whose first business was helping her new husband to make household improvements

including building a wooden floor and providing them with a wooden door and a real window! She was a fair mother and always loved Lincoln and Sarah as her own children.

Though she herself could not read, she heard from Thomas about Lincoln's efforts to read. Hence, she brought with her six books. Among them were 'Pilgrim's Progress', 'Parson Weem's Life of Washington' and 'Aesop's Fables'.

Though the family had little money for paper, pencils or books, Sarah did what she could to get a few things so that Lincoln could read and write. Neighbours recalled how Lincoln would walk for miles to borrow a book!

A second opportunity for the children to attend school occurred after Sarah arrived, and she, too, saw the importance of it. The school was only a mile away but it lasted for just three months.

As time passed, Lincoln grew into a tall and strong man, and his father often hired him out to work for neighbours. There weren't many schools and with much work load Lincoln could hardly attend school for a year altogether. By the age of 15, he learnt to read which was sufficient for him to teach himself whatever he wanted. He would read

by the light of fireplace and read every book he could get from his neighbours and friends.

It took him long to finish a book but he would leave the book only after making sure he understood it completely. People thought he was slow, but his mother understood and encouraged him.

Thomas neither understood nor encouraged his son's intellectual ambitions. He would often scold Lincoln for preferring reading over working. Lincoln never wanted to be a farmer like his father. He wanted to explore various possibilities for himself.

In 1828, with one of his friends, Lincoln took a flatboat loaded with farm produce down the Ohio and Mississippi rivers to New Orleans.

Lincoln's father moved his family to Illinois, where he built a cabin on the Sangamon River. Within a year, the family again moved, in Illinois only, just west of Decatur. Lincoln built a second flatboat and made another run down the river, but this time on his own. With his earnings he moved to the town of New Salem, Illinois in 1831. He was 21 at that time.

These trips widened his horizons and his vision. He was shocked to see men and women being bought and sold in the slave markets of New Orleans.

The Turning Point

Life in New Salem was a turning point for Lincoln, and the great man of history began to emerge from this very point.

As a young man, Lincoln stood out from the crowd, tall and lanky at six-foot four-inches with sharp features and unruly coarse black hair.

He took up a job as a clerk in a general store. During those times, a general store was a meeting place, and Lincoln was witty, intelligent and honest. He loved telling funny stories. Soon he became a popular member of the town, amongst the locals of all kinds who came to the store to talk and trade and to enjoy his stories. The members of the New Salem Debating Society welcomed him, and Lincoln began to develop his skills as a convincing speaker.

Lincoln's six years in New Salem were crucial. He worked in many types of profiles like a store clerk, a mill hand, as a partner in a general store which failed, as a postmaster and even as a surveyor. He grew in experience and knowledge. Although usually Lincoln was jovial and loved to tell stories to crowds, sometimes he would become very sad and would sit alone, lost in deep thoughts. He never discussed the cause of his sadness with anyone. He also suffered from bouts of depression.

Six months after his arrival in town, Lincoln developed an interest in politics and announced that he was joining as a candidate for a seat in the Illinois state legislature. A few weeks later, the Black Hawk War broke out. Lincoln volunteered for the militia and was elected as the captain of his company. As a soldier, Lincoln could not campaign for office.

He lost the election, but received 92 percent of the vote in the New Salem district. He decided to run for the state legislature again and to win over the farmers as he had worked with them for harvesting in the fields. This time Lincoln won.

Moving Towards Success

John Todd Stuart, who was a leader of the Whigs, was also an outstanding lawyer. Impressed with Lincoln's campaigning skills, Stuart inspired and guided him to study law. In 1836, Lincoln obtained his license and a year later he moved to Springfield and became Stuart's partner.

Springfield was a little frontier town with log cabins. For Lincoln, however, it was the biggest place he had ever lived in. It even had a book-store! Lincoln used to wear a tall stovepipe hat in which he would carry important papers as he would lose them sometimes.

There was not enough business in Springfield so Lincoln had to travel a lot. He had to stay in small, rough inns, sometimes sleep on the floors and had to walk long distances.

He did not resent the hard life as he loved meeting different people. These people, in turn, were much impressed with his friendliness, honesty and the funny stories he would narrate.

Lincoln was a strong supporter of the Whig Party. He worked hard in the Whig political

functions, and became one of the most important members in Illinois.

He served four straight terms in the legislature, emerging as a party leader. Popular among people owing to his friendly and jovial personality, Lincoln was quite shy and uncomfortable with women. He was doubtful of getting married ever.

However, at a party, he met Mary Todd. Daughter of a well-to-do banker, she was pretty, cultured and well educated. She liked Lincoln and seeing his discomfort tried to put him at ease by doing most of the talking herself.

Interested in politics, she would often say that she would marry the man who would be president. Little did she know that she had predicted Lincoln's future!

The two were married in 1842. Lincoln bought a small house with basic amenities. They had four sons—Robert, Edward, Willie and Thomas. Edward died when he was three.

Since Lincoln had to be away from home for weeks together due to his legal commitments, Mary had to cope up with household management and bringing up children alone.

However, both the parents never scolded their children to regulate their behaviour and let them do whatever they wanted, even in Lincoln's law office.

Lincoln wanted to do something for his country and not only for his county. To achieve his goal, he wanted the candidature of the Whig party for the United States House of Representatives. The party chose another candidate but Lincoln kept his spirit high and worked extremely hard to get his rival elected. And his hard work paid well!

In 1846, Lincoln was elected as a representative from Illinois. He shifted to Washington D.C. with his family.

Working very hard, he never missed a session of Congress, served the committees and very sincerely went about all the chores. However, he went unnoticed as he did not achieve anything spectacular. His term finished after two years and he returned to Springfield disheartened with politics. He gave full time to his law practice and became one of the leading lawyers in the state.

While Lincoln rebuilt his legal career, the nation was on the verge of getting divided. New territories were added to United States in the Mexican War. The issue of slavery had raised its ugly head. The Southerners demanded the security and rights of slavery everywhere whereas the Northerners wanted it abolished. A national crisis soon became imminent.

The Skilled Debater

Lincoln's return to politics happened largely due the Kansas-Nebraska Act in 1854.

It had been decided by the Congress in 1820 that slavery would not be allowed beyond Missouri in the north.

However, the Kansas-Nebraska Act drafted by Stephen A. Douglas, the senator of Illinois, violated the decision of the Congress. It left the decision of slavery up to the new territories; they could legalize it.

Lincoln passionately opposed slavery. He strongly believed that slavery was morally, socially and politically wrong and wanted it abolished.

However, as much as he hated slavery, he was afraid that since it was legalized by the constitution, its abolition would lead to violence. He believed that if it was allowed only in states where it already was legal and was not allowed in new territories, eventually it would die out as people will realize that it was bad for the country. So, he supported the legal rights of the slaves.

In 1855, Lincoln filed for nomination as senator but his failure convinced him that the Whig party was dead and in 1856 he joined the new Republican Party. Lincoln quickly emerged as an outstanding leader of the new party. Although he was not chosen for the candidature of vice-president, he was recognized as an important national figure.

Lincoln followed Senator Stephen Douglas, the candidate of the Democratic Party, to Springfield where in an open-air speech Douglas said that it is the people in every state who should decide whether they wanted slavery or not. Lincoln announced that the next day he would prove Douglas wrong.

A huge audience awaited him the next day. Lincoln spoke for three hours advocating equal rights for the African-Americans in America as the country was founded on the belief that no one had the right to govern another without consent!

Lincoln again challenged Douglas to a series of debates. Douglas accepted, and the two met in seven, three-hour long debates in every part of the state.

Both men were shrewd debaters. However, Lincoln's speeches were eloquent and powerful. Douglas insisted that slavery could exist in half the country as it had for 70 years. On the other hand, Lincoln wanted to be declared in the 'Declaration of Independence' life, liberty and happiness for the African-Americans.

Lincoln quoted from Mark's gospel in the Bible and gave one of his most famous speeches. He said, "A house divided against itself cannot stand. I believe the government cannot endure permanently half slave and half free. I do not expect the Union to be dissolved—I do not expect the house to fall—but I do expect it will cease to be divided. It will become all one thing, or all the other."

Although Douglas was re-elected as senator, Lincoln had gained national attention and his name was soon mentioned for presidency.

Election as President

Lincoln's prospects were enhanced by the favourable impact of his speech on a large crowd in New York City in 1860. This resulted in Lincoln receiving numerous invitations to speak and he travelled extensively.

Lincoln's speeches focused on the Republican value system, according to which all work in a free society was honorable. He compared slavery to bondage. He spoke about his humble beginnings as a hired labourer who had mauled rails, worked on a flat-boat—'just what might happen to any poor man's son.'

He believed that people can rise in life and that every man should be given equal opportunity.

When Lincoln won the election, an 11-year-old girl named Grace Bedell wrote the President-elect a letter: "You would look a great deal better if you grew a beard for your face is so thin. All the ladies like whiskers and they would tease their husbands to vote for you and then you would be President."

Lincoln took her advice, and his beard was born! Lincoln later visited the little girl and told her, "Gracie, look at my whiskers. I have been growing them for you."

With the Republicans united, the Democrats divided, and with a total of four candidates, in the election on November 6, Lincoln won. Mary was delighted as she had finally become the wife of a President.

Lincoln had a sleepless night as he realized the great responsibility he had on his shoulders. With only one year of schooling and almost negligible experience in the national government, he did not know much about the working of a President.

A Divided Nation

Lincoln was greeted with hatred by the slave states upon his election as the President. Refusing to recognize Lincoln as their President, seven states seceded from the Union. Four more states joined them and together, these eleven states declared themselves as 'Confederate States of America' electing Jefferson Davis as their President.

In his inaugural address, Lincoln clarified his position on the national situation. He maintained that secession was wrong, and the Union could not legally be broken apart.

He declared that he would not let the nation to be divided into two countries. He did not talk about slavery in the states, as four states where slavery was legal—Delaware, Maryland, Kentucky and Missouri—had not left the Union.

A lot of compromise proposals emerged during the 1860-1861 session of Congress but for most secessionists there was no turning back.

Lincoln hoped that his inaugural address would enable the seven states to "reconstruct" themselves back into the Union. But the day after his inauguration, Lincoln learned that the Confederate leaders demanded the transfer of Fort Sumter in South Carolina, which was a part of the Union, to the Confederacy. Lincoln did not agree to it.

A month later, on April 12, 1861, the soldiers of the Confederacy opened fire on the soldiers of the Union at Fort Sumter. Lincoln was determined to preserve the Union, so he decided to take a stand against the Confederacy and Sumter. After the firing on Fort Sumter, Lincoln called upon the state governors for troops and proclaimed a blockade of the Southern ports. However, he still needed a strategic plan to carry out the expedition.

So, he insisted on a policy of unconditional surrender as Sovereignty was not negotiable.

As a war leader, Lincoln built up the army and spent money on weapons. The Northerners eagerly volunteered to be recruited in the army as they thought the war would end soon. Lincoln oversaw everything himself.

But the war did not end soon. From 1861 to 1864, Lincoln

tried a succession of commanders for the army in Virginia but was disappointed by all. People became impatient and began doubting his abilities as President.

While Lincoln was learning to be an effective President, his family was settling into the White House—their new home. The White House, however, was in a pitiable state. Mary was given some money to renovate it but

she overspent it in her effort to make the house elegant and beautiful. She was rebuked severely by Lincoln, who rarely lost his temper. Money was required at this time for fulfilling the needs of the army.

Lincoln's sons, Willie and Tad enjoyed their time in Washington. They made friends with the guards in the White House and did whatever they wanted without being apprehended by their parents. The boys would barge into Lincoln's office while he would be discussing serious matters. Lincoln did not mind this intrusion as they would make him smile in such difficult times of war and distress.

The Lincolns were not appreciated by the people for this as they felt that the boys were spoiled too much by their parents.

Lincoln, in fact, would also not stop visitors who came to meet him and request him for favours. He would, as much as he could, try to grant these requests.

His compassion won the hearts of the people and they referred to him as 'Father Abraham.' The nation's sympathy increased more for him when his 11-year-old son, Willie, died of typhoid in 1862. Lincoln was so grief-stricken by his son's death that sometimes he would lock himself in his room and weep bitterly. Mary too was shattered by the death of her son.

End Of Slavery

The situation of America became grim with passing time. No one had thought that the war would carry on for so long. Thousands of men were killed and wounded on both sides. The government was unable to bear the expenses of the continuing war.

The South was fighting the war to keep slavery intact, whereas the abolitionists supported the war hoping to put an end to slavery by declaring it illegal. Lincoln felt trapped as he had sworn to protect the laws of the United States and slavery was legal in the Southern states. There were some people in the North, who disagreed to slavery being abolished by law, and Lincoln feared that by doing so he might lose the support of abolitionists.

He knew that he alone could not change the laws in the Constitution; it had to come from the people.

Finally, in response to the rising anti-slavery sentiment, Lincoln devised a preliminary emancipation plan of his own. According to it, the slaves were to be freed by state action, slave holders were to be compensated, the federal government was to share the financial burden, and the emancipation process was to be gradual.

A law was eventually passed by the Congress to free the slaves captured by the Union army.

According to the final Emancipation Proclamation, which was an act of war applying to the confederate states only, all the slaves were to be freed in the rebel states except for Delaware, Maryland, Missouri and Kentucky since these states had stayed with the Union. Here legal slavery would be recognized.

England and Europe supported the cause of the Union.

The Proclamation, however, could not be enforced without winning the war.

As President of the United States, Lincoln was at first reluctant to adopt an abolitionist policy. He was concerned about the possible difficulties of incorporating nearly four million African-Americans, once freed, into the nation's social and political life.

Nevertheless, he was determined to end slavery for good. He held discussions with his cabinet and told them about his decision. The act took effect on January 1, 1863. The news was heard and many slaves escaped to the North overnight. These slaves were taken in the Union army and regiments of black soldiers were formed.

The Proclamation brought freedom during the war to about 200,000 slaves.

Slowly but steadily, one by one the states acted favourably on it. Lincoln had thus managed to keep the nation united while also bringing about an end to slavery.

However, the war was still raging and needed to end.

The Gettysburg Address

Lincoln trusted Henry W. Halleck, a general in chief who advised him to give the command of the Federal forces in the hands of Ulysses S. Grant, a competent general. He already had important victories to talk of. For the first time, Lincoln had a commanding general in whom he had full confidence—one who could take from his shoulders some of the burden of constant military oversight.

Lincoln willingly gave him freedom to take the necessary decisions and action. Grant planned simultaneous attacks by the Union army on several fronts to prevent Confederates from shifting troops from one point to another.

Many bloody battles were fought in quick succession to destroy railroads and factories to cripple the movement of the Confederate army. The long war had wearied the people and now they were unwilling to volunteer to be enrolled in the army. As a consequence, a draft was issued and men were forced to enlist in the army. There was uproar and New York blazed with riots. People could hardly see any reason in dying for the freedom of black people.

They started turning against Lincoln and demanded his explanation. The opportunity to address the nation came when the Union Army won the Battle of Gettysburg. Thousands of soldiers had been killed on both the sides and a special cemetery had been created to bury them all; the commemoration was held on November 19, 1863.

Lincoln's speech at Gettysburg is known as a landmark speech in the history of America. His opening sentence was a quote from the Declaration of Independence: "All men are created equal." He reminded the audience that the idea of equality was the foundation of the United States. No other country was based on this principle and he could under no circumstances bow down to the demands of the rebels.

The Union was not only fighting to keep the United States united but to also secure the very essence of democratic principles of 'government of the people, by the people and for the people.'

The listeners were too stunned to even clap at the end of the speech. There was complete silence. He had struck a chord in the hearts of people with his loyalty and passion for the guiding principles of the Constitution of United States.

The war continued, without an end in sight.

The Victory

To win the war, President Lincoln had to have popular support. The opposition party remained alive and strong. Within his own party, Lincoln had to face opposition.

He had to deal with even more serious factional uprisings in the Congress. The big issue was the 'reconstruction' of the South. The seceded states of Louisiana, Arkansas and Tennessee had been largely recovered by the Union armies.

In 1863, Lincoln proposed his 'ten percent plan'. According to it, the Confederates would be given pardon for their war actions if they pledged loyalty to the Union. This plan also intended that the new state governments should abolish slavery.

Lincoln's first term as the President was nearing end in 1864, and elections were approaching. He was advised to put off the elections but Lincoln did not agree as he felt that it would not be possible to have a free government without elections. Though he was re-nominated as the presidential candidate by the Republican Party, they were unanimously opposed and hated him beneath the surface on Reconstruction.

Americans were fed up with the war. Lincoln came under immense pressure to open peace negotiations. The people of America were willing to vote for anyone who could rid them of further war. Lincoln knew that the soldiers supported him and he ensured that they could vote. However, he was unsure of his victory.

Two months before the election, news of huge victories started pouring in and overnight peoples' opinion tilted in favour of Lincoln. His tarnished reputation as commander-in-chief became lustrous now.

He was triumphantly re-elected in November, carrying every Union state except New Jersey, Delaware and Kentucky.

By the beginning of 1865, it became certain that the war was about to end. Grant captured Richmond in March and cornered the troops of General Robert E. Lee of the Confederate army. The latter surrendered to Grant in April. The war was over for all practical purposes.

In his second inaugural address, Lincoln looked forward to a peace "with malice toward none; with charity for all." He also suggested that "this terrible war" may have been God's punishment of the whole nation for the wrong of slavery.

After Lee's surrender, Lincoln spoke to the excited crowd cheering at the White House on April 11. He hinted that his Reconstruction policy would enfranchise literate blacks and black army veterans.

However, in the crowd there were standing John Wilkes Booth and his friends.

A native of Maryland and an unstable egoist who supported the Confederacy and hated Lincoln, Booth headed a shadowy conspiracy with links to the Confederate secret service, which had intended to kidnap Lincoln and hold him hostage in Richmond. The fall of Richmond had ruined that plot, so Booth decided to kill the President. At the end of the war, Lincoln's policy for the defeated South was not clear, though he continued to believe that the main object should be to restore the "seceded states" to the Union as soon as possible. On April 14, 1865, a month after his second term began, the Lincolns went to watch a comedy at Ford's Theatre in Washington, D.C.

Booth came to know of this and he planned to execute his intention. He was familiar with the building and easily gained entrance to their box. He shot Lincoln in the head. Lincoln died at 7:22 the next morning. He was 56 years old.

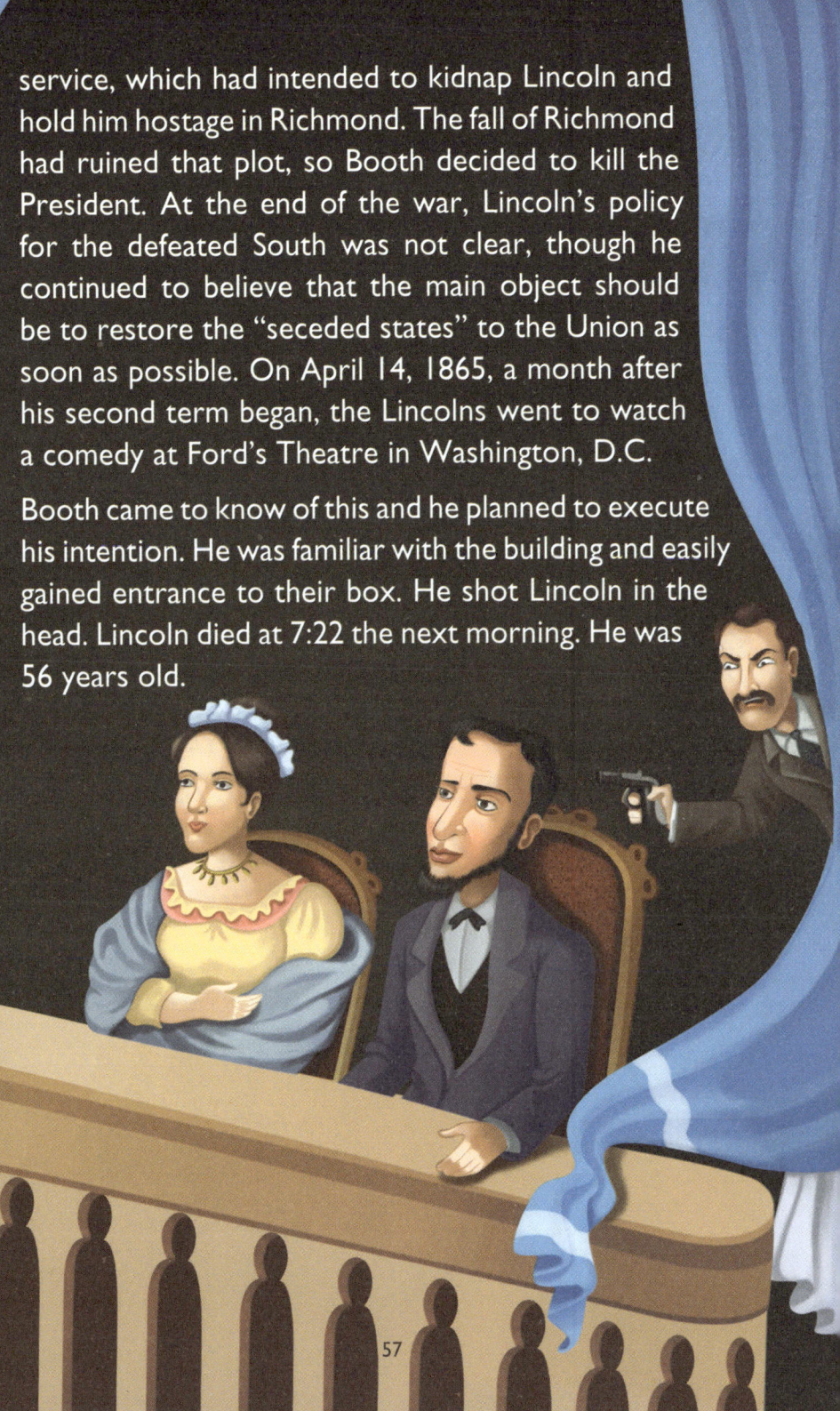

The Last Journey

Lincoln's assassination left the entire nation in deep shock and mourning. Clocks were stopped to mark the moment of his death. Millions of people flocked to Washington D.C. to pay their homage to him.

Lincoln's body was carried to Springfield on a special train for burial. Scores of people waited for long hours at the stoppages to bid good-bye and catch a last glimpse of their beloved President.

Mary Lincoln was too traumatized to recover from the shock of her husband's death.

John Wilkes Booth went into hiding. He was hunted down and while trying to escape, he was shot to death.

Scorned and ridiculed by many critics during his presidency, today Lincoln is more honoured than any other President except for probably George Washington. He is remembered along with George Washington on Presidents' Day. His words and deeds continue to live in people's memories even today.

Many cities, counties, national parks and mountains have been named after him. He was an extraordinary man who determinedly kept his country together, worked sincerely towards abolition of slavery while upholding the Constitution in its glory. He is rightly called the greatest President of America.

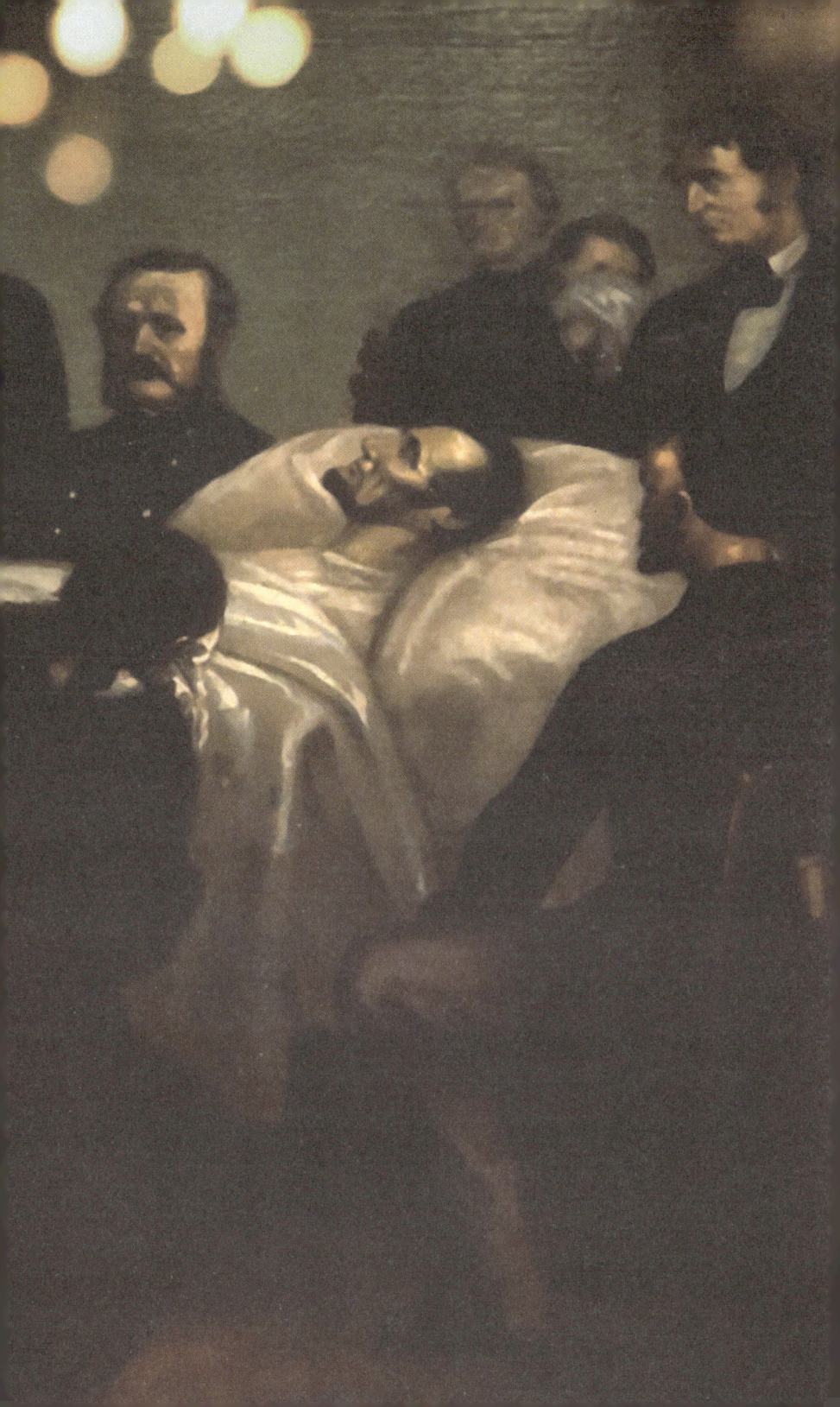

Timeline

- **1809** Abraham Lincoln is born in Hardin County, Kentucky, near Hodgenville
- **1816** The Lincoln family relocates to the frontier of Indiana
- **1818** Lincoln's mother, Nancy Hanks Lincoln, dies of milk sickness
- **1819** Lincoln's father, Thomas Lincoln, remarries widow Sarah Bush Johnston
- **1820** Missouri Compromise sets boundary line between free and slave territory
- **1828** Lincoln works on cargo flatboat bound for New Orleans
- **1830** The Lincoln family relocates to Illinois, settling along Sangamon River
- **1831** Lincoln makes second flatboat trip to New Orleans
- **1831** He separates from his family, moving to New Salem, Illinois
- **1832** Lincoln serves as captain of volunteer company in Black Hawk War

    The same year, he loses bid for Illinois State Legislature

- 1834 Lincoln gets elected to Illinois State Legislature at age 24
- 1835 Ann Rutledge dies
- 1836 Lincoln gets re-elected to Illinois state legislature
- 1837 He is admitted to the bar in Illinois; begins practicing law
- 1837 He relocates to Springfield after state capital is moved there
- 1837 He forms law partnership with John T. Stuart
- 1838 Lincoln gets re-elected to Illinois State Legislature for a third term
- 1840 He gets re-elected to Illinois State Legislature for a fourth term

    He gets engaged to Mary Todd
- 1841 Lincoln forms law partnership with Stephen T. Logan
- 1842 He decides not to seek fifth term in Illinois State Legislature

    The same year, he is challenged to duel by James Shields, which is later called off

Timeline

- Lincoln marries Mary Todd in an Episcopalian Service in Springfield

- **1843** Lincoln fails to obtain Whig nomination for U.S. Congress

  Mary Todd Lincoln gives birth to their eldest son, Robert Todd

- **1844** Lincoln buys a farm house in Springfield

- **1846** Lincoln gets elected to U.S. Congress as Whig Representative from Illinois

- **1847** Lincoln family leaves Springfield for Washington

  Lincoln presents at convocation of Thirtieth Congress

- **1849** He introduces gradual emancipation bill for slaves in District of Columbia

  He completes term in Washington and returns to Springfield to practice law

  Later that year, he fails to secure position as commissioner of General Land Office

- **1850** His son, Edward Lincoln, dies after prolonged illness

  The same year, Omnibus Compromise of 1850 signed into law

Lincoln's third son William Wallace is born

- 1853 His fourth son, Thomas 'Tad' is born
- 1854 Kansas-Nebraska Act becomes law, nullifying Missouri Compromise

  Lincoln is elected to Illinois state legislature; declines seat to run for U.S. Senate

- 1856 Lincoln attends first Republican national convention in Philadelphia; receives considerable support for vice-presidential nomination

- 1858 He receives Republican nomination for U.S. Senate; delivers famous 'house divided' speech

  He participates in a series of debates with incumbent Senator Stephen Douglas

  He loses Senate bid once again

- 1859 John Brown leads raid on Harper's Ferry, Virginia

- 1860 Lincoln delivers speech at Cooper Institute, New York City

  Democratic convention in Charleston, South Carolina fractures

Timeline

Lincoln receives nomination for president at Republican convention in Chicago

He is elected 16th President of the United States

- **1861** Lincoln inaugurated in Washington, delivers First Inaugural Address

    He orders reinforcements sent to Fort Sumter

    Confederate forces open fire on Fort Sumter, beginning Civil War

    Lincoln proclaims blockade against Southern ports

    Congress grants Lincoln considerable war powers

- **1862** Lincoln's son, William Wallace Lincoln, dies

    Ironclad warships Monitor and Virginia battle to a draw

    Lincoln takes supreme command of Union forces; McClellan begins Peninsular Campaign on Richmond

    Battle of Shiloh in Tennessee results in heavy losses for both sides

Lincoln signs act abolishing slavery in District of Columbia

Slavery is prohibited in United States territories

1863 Emancipation Proclamation goes into effect

Lincoln names U.S. Grant to command Union forces in the west

Union forces victorious at Battle of Gettysburg

Lincoln delivers Gettysburg Address

Union forces seize Chattanooga

Grant assumes command of all Union forces; William Tecumseh Sherman takes control in western theater

Lincoln is nominated for President by National Union Party

Grant digs in for nine-month siege of Petersburg

Lincoln calls for 500,000 more volunteers

Democrats nominate McClellan for president on peace platform

Timeline

- **1865** •Grant's forces break Confederate defensive and march on Richmond

    Lincoln visits destruction at Richmond

    Lee surrenders to Grant near Appomattox Court House, Virginia

    Lincoln makes last public speech, concerning question of reconstruction

    Lincoln fatally shot by John Wilkes Booth while attending play at Ford's Theater, Washington, D.C.

    Lincoln dies at 7:22 a.m. from complications caused by gunshot wound

- **1865** Lincoln interred at Oak Ridge Cemetery, near Springfield, Illinois

Group Discussion

What is your idea about slavery? Who are slaves? In which parts of the world was slavery practiced? Discuss with your teacher in the class. Take notes of the points you have learnt.

Project Work

Search the Internet and get information about the most famous Presidents of America. Write a short paragraph on each of them and paste their pictures. You may restrict your search to 5/6 names.

Pair and Share

Tell your partner what you know about Abraham Lincoln. Make notes with each other's points.

Questions

1. Where was Lincoln born?
2. Name his parents.
3. How many brothers and sisters did he have? Name them.
4. Due to the land dispute, where did Lincoln and his family shift to?

Activities

5. How did his mother die? How old was Lincoln then?

6. What was Lincoln's step-mother's name?

7. Name the three books she had brought for Lincoln.

8. When did Lincoln come to know about slavery?

9. Which quality in Lincoln's character attracted people the most?

10. Who inspired and guided Lincoln to study law?

11. Why did Lincoln wear a stove pipe hat?

12. What was the name of his wife?

13. Which procedure did Lincoln object to and he strongly opposed?

14. When Lincoln became the 16th President of United States of America, why did some people form a dislike for him?

15. How did Lincoln die?

16. How did slavery end?

abandoned: deserted or left alone

abolished: to formally put an end to a system or practice

abolition: the action of abolishing a system or practice

abolitionist: a person who favours the abolition of a practice or institution

ambitions: a strong desire to achieve something

anti-slavery: opposed to the practice of slavery

appreciate: recognize the full worth of

audience: assembled spectators or listeners at a public event

campaigning: an organized course of action to achieve something

candidate: a person who applies for a job or is nominated for elections

coarse: rough in texture

commitments: the state of being dedicated to a cause or activity

community: a group of people living in the same place or having a few characteristics in common

compensate: to give someone money or something to fill a loss

confederate: a person one works with, especially in something secret or illegal; an accomplice

Glossary

conspiracy: a secret plan made by a group to do something harmful

depression: feelings of severe despondency

discomfort: something that makes one feel uncomfortable

disheartened: to lose determination or confidence

distinctive: a distinguishing characteristic of a person or thing

drafted: a preliminary version of a piece of writing

egoist: a person who is excessively absorbed in themselves

eloquent: fluent in speaking or writing

emancipation: the process of being free from legal, social, or political restrictions

emancipator: a person who helps someone to be free from some authority

encourage: give support and confidence to someone

expedition: a journey undertaken by a group of people with a purpose of exploration

frontier: a border separating two countries

grief: intense sorrow

hostage: a person seized or held as security for the fulfillment of some condition

humble: showing low estimate of one's importance

inauguration: the introduction of a system

lanky: awkwardly thin and tall

license: to authorize the use or release of something

mourn: to feel and show sorrow for the death of someone

negligible: very less

opportunity: a set of circumstances that makes it possible to do something

opposed: to be against somebody or something

pioneer: a person who is among the first to explore or settle a new area

plunge: to jump into something

proclamation: a public or official announcement regarding a matter of great importance

rebellious: a person who resists the authority of someone or something

rebuke: to express sharp disapproval for someone distress: extreme anxiety, sorrow, or pain

recognize: to identify someone or something from having encountered them before

reputation: the opinion about someone or

Glossary

Glossary

resent: to feel bitterness or indignation in a circumstance, action, or towards a person

secession: the action of withdrawing formally from membership of an association

simultaneous: occurring, or done at the same time

slavery: the practice of owning slaves or bonded labour

something inaugural: the beginning of an institution or activity

spectacular: beautiful and eye-catching

strategist: a person skilled in planning during the war or in politics

succession: a number of people or things of a similar kind following one after the other

surrender: to submit to some authority

surveyor: a person who examines the condition of land and buildings capably

tarnish: to lose good will

terrible: extremely unpleasant

violence: behaviour involving physical force intended to hurt, damage, or kill someone

volunteer: a person who freely takes part in a task

wearied: extreme tiredness

whiskers: a long projecting hair or bristle growing from the face